Sand, Sea & Cross Stitch

Anna Field

Sand, Sea
& Cross Stitch

Photographs by Frédéric Lucano
Styling by Lise Meunier

D&C
David and Charles

www.stitchcraftcreate.co.uk

Because I live in Paris, I sometimes have a craving for sand and sea air!

I've conceived this book as a postcard sent from New England, where I spent some wonderful years when I was a student. I have happy memories of white in the house to brighten up stormy days, wood everywhere to create a warm interior, birds, and salt wind in my hair. I acquired a taste for authenticity, calm and infinite landscapes there. I also love the primary colours of flags and boats, and beaches that stretch for miles; that special charm of the East Coast of the United States that *la maison sur le quai* has successfully transposed to the Normandy coast.

We shot the photographs for this book there; but follow me, soak up the atmosphere, and you'll find yourself on the other side of the Atlantic!

Contents

Getting started

Before you begin to cross stitch, make sure that your fabric is prepared so that it doesn't fray while you're working on it. You can do this by either overstitching it using large tacking (basting) stitches, or simply applying strips of low-tack masking tape around the edge of your work. In all cases, the piece of fabric you use will need to be larger than the design that you want to cross stitch. Allow a margin of 10–15cm (4–6in) on each side of the design.

Fold your fabric in four to find the centre of your work. Make some tacking (basting) stitches along the horizontal and vertical folds. These will provide you with guidelines when you begin cross stitching. Next, find the central point on the chart of the design you want to cross stitch. Begin your cross stitch here, making your first stitch in the centre of your fabric. Once you have made the first cross stitches, you can remove the tacking (basting) stitches.

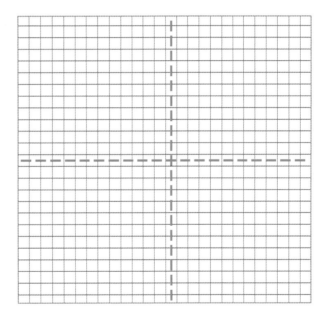

Use an embroidery frame to ensure that your stitches are even. Stretch your fabric over the frame, being careful to move it regularly so that the fabric doesn't become damaged. Alternatively, you can wrap a length of ribbon around the inner part of the frame, which will prevent the wood of the frame from marking or tearing the fabric.

If your piece of fabric is too small for your embroidery frame, tack a few scraps of fabric of the same quality and thickness along the four sides of your cross stitch canvas, then stretch the whole piece over the frame in the same way as usual.

For each of the designs, we have indicated the type of fabric and the number of threads we used. However, there's nothing to stop you from using a different quality or weave of fabric. Make a small sample with a few stitches to work out the number of strands of embroidery thread (floss) you will need for the fabric you have chosen.

A test piece like this is useful for all types of embroidery. Stranded embroidery thread (floss) is made up of six strands. Cut lengths of thread of about 40cm (16in). As a general rule, for an Aida canvas of 5.5 stitches per centimetre (14 count), you will need two or three strands of embroidery thread; for a linen canvas with 11 or 12 threads per centimetre (28 or 30 count), you will need to work with two strands of thread over two threads of warp and weft. However, if you want to cross stitch over a single thread of warp and weft, use a single strand of embroidery thread.

When you begin, take a 1m (40in) length a single strand of thread. Fold it in half and begin the first diagonal of the first stitch by passing the needle into the loop from the other side. Pull gently to secure the thread. If your length of thread becomes tangled, turn the work over and let your needle dangle. The strands will soon untangle by themselves.

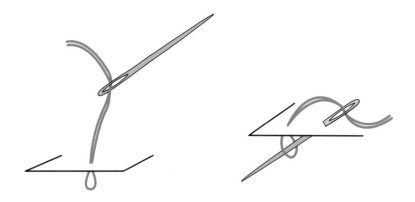

Change your thread as soon as you have finished a series of stitches. Don't leave long threads hanging at the back of your cross stitch as they may show through once you've framed the piece and will also make it bulky. However, if the colours are very close, you could stitch with the threads at the same time. Make a few stitches using colour A, pass the needle through to the right side of the work and leave it over the area you've just stitched. Make a few stitches with colour B, leave it on the right side of the fabric and continue with colour A, threading the needle under the B stitches on the reverse side of the work.

When you have finished, thread your needle under the three or four last stitches. That way you will avoid having to tie knots on the back of your work that will create unsightly lumps that may be visible once you've framed your cross stitch piece.

To cross stitch the designs in this book, you will need only cross stitch and its derivatives, all of which are very easy to execute.

 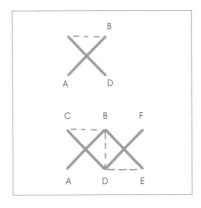 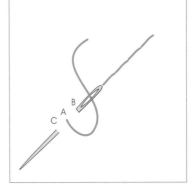

Cross stitch

1 Bring the needle up at A, insert it at B, then bring it up again at C. Insert at D, bring up at E.

2 Repeat in the opposite direction. From E, insert at B to form a cross.

Alternative cross stitch

1 Bring the needle up at A, insert it at B, bring it up again at C and insert at D.

2 Bring it up again at B, insert at E, bring it up at D and insert at F so as to make a cross stitch on the front. The threads are reversed from the first cross stitch and the back forms a crenellated pattern.

Backstitch

Bring the needle up at A and insert at B. Bring the needle up again at C. The AB stitch should be the same length as the CA one.

To cross stitch these designs, we recommend a range of 24 colours. However, there's no reason why you can't switch around the colours or even cross stitch the designs using a single colour. Let your imagination have free rein!

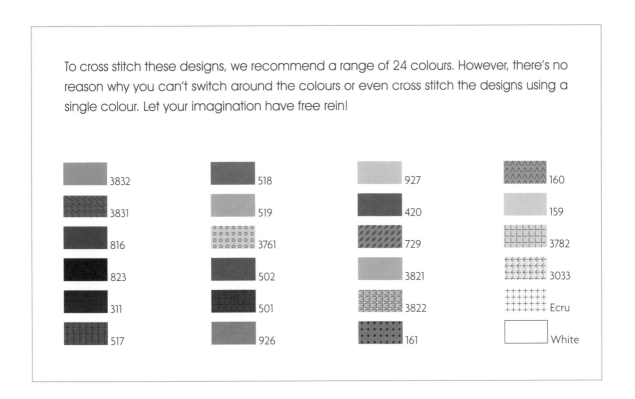

3832	518	927	160
3831	519	420	159
816	3761	729	3782
823	502	3821	3033
311	501	3822	Ecru
517	926	161	White

Visitors' book (details) charts page 18, instructions page 133

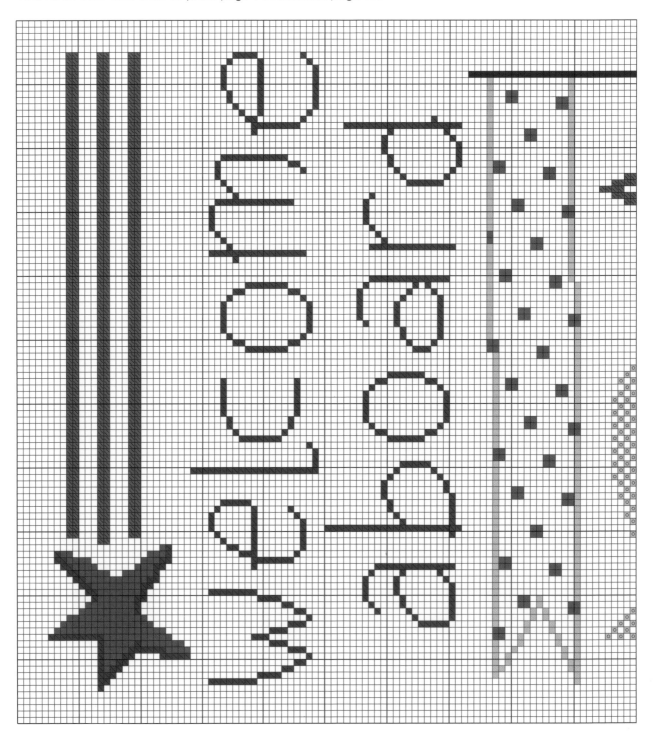

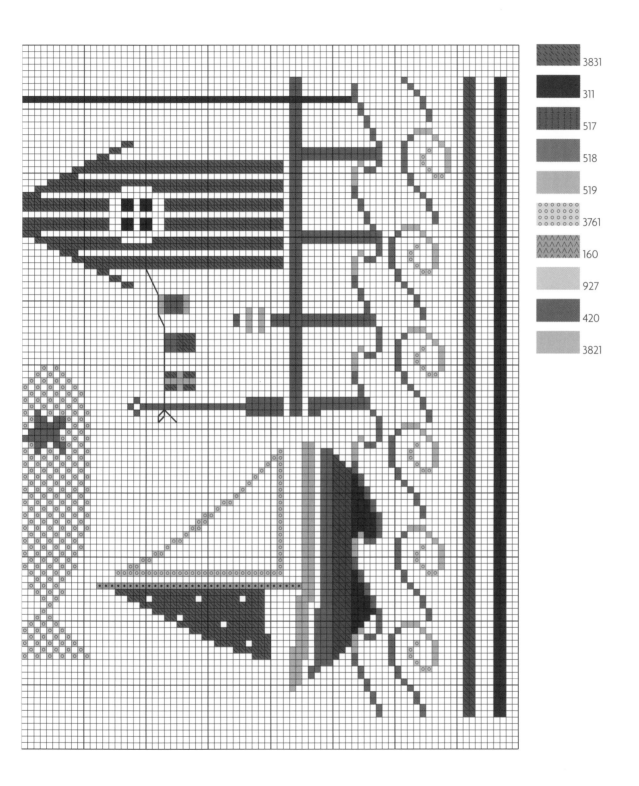

	3831
	311
	517
	518
	519
	3761
	160
	927
	420
	3821

Visitors' book (details) photo page 15, instructions page 133

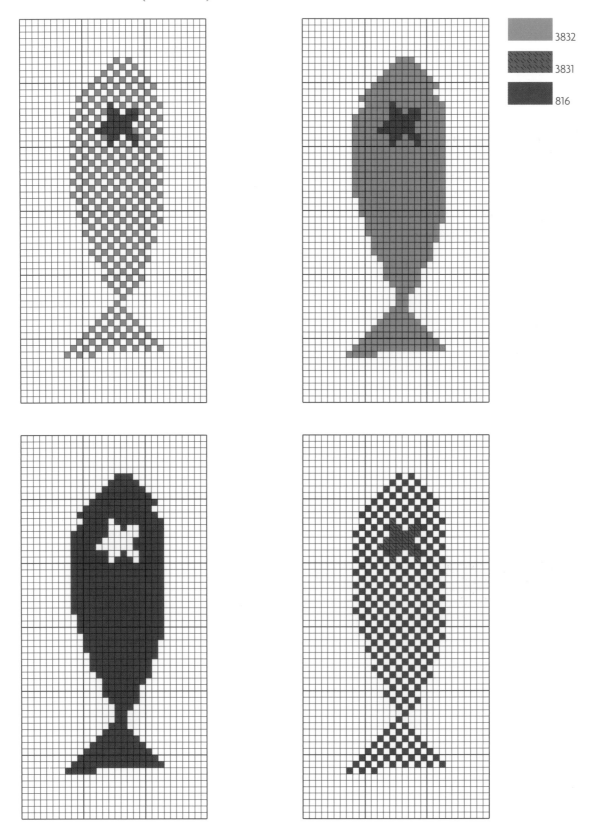

3832
3831
816

	3831
	311
	517
	518
	519
	3761
	502
	501
	161
	160
	159

On the seaside chart pages 22–23, instructions page 133

	3832
	3831
	816
	311
	517
	518
	519
	3761
	927
	161
	160
	159

S for … charts pages 26–28, instructions page 134

Surf photos pages 24–25 and 32, instructions page 134

Sand photos pages 24–25 and 32, instructions page 134

Sail photos pages 24–25, instructions page 134

Swimming photo pages 24–25, instructions page 134

	3832
	3831
	816
	823
	311
	517
	518
	519
	3761
	420
	729
	3821
	3822
	161
	160
	159
	White

Sea photos pages 30–31 and 32, instructions page 134

Sun photo pages 30–31 and 32, instructions page 134

Shell photos pages 30–31 and 32, instructions page 134

Ship photos pages 30–31 and 32, instructions page 134

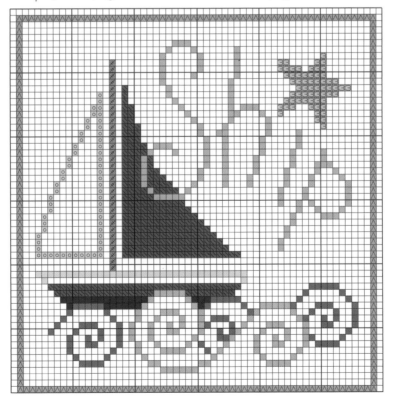

	3832
	3831
	816
	823
	311
	517
	518
	519
	3761
	420
	729
	3821
	3822
	161
	160
	159
	White

Little message (detail) chart page 28, instructions page 134

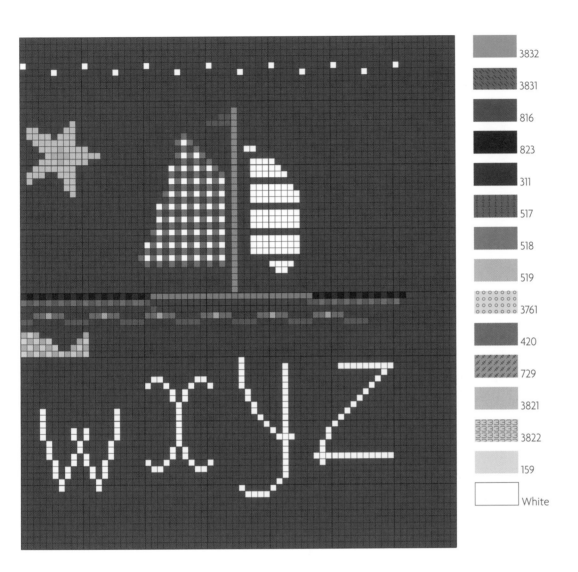

Color	Code
	3832
	3831
	816
	823
	311
	517
	518
	519
	3761
	420
	729
	3821
	3822
	159
	White

Placement diagram

I love sea chart pages 44–45, instructions pages 134–135

816

311

White

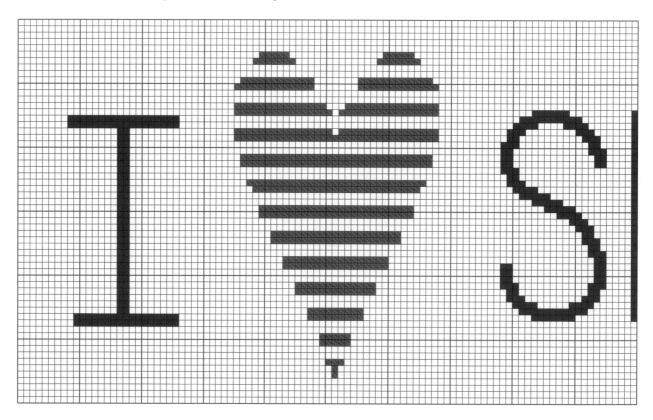

With such a simple chart, feel free to tranpose or change the colours, use a different fabric or adapt the motifs.

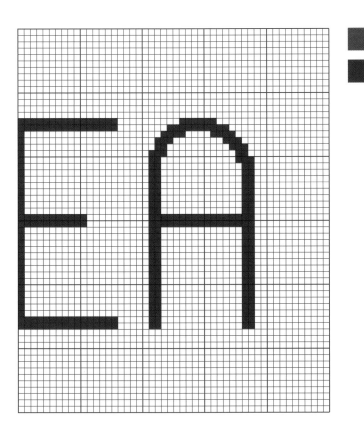

816

311

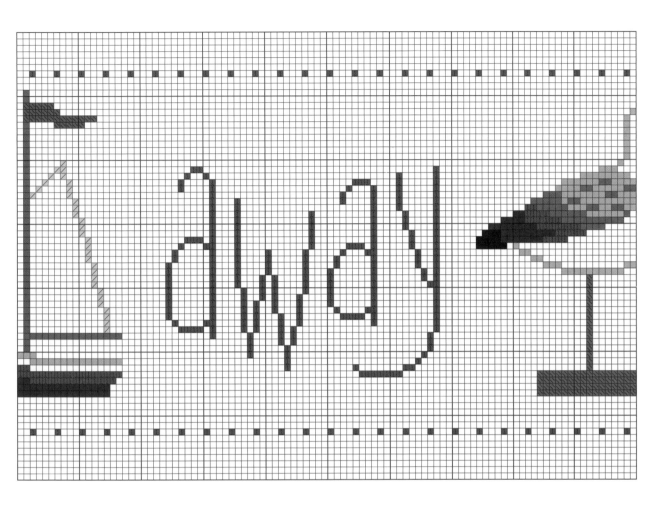

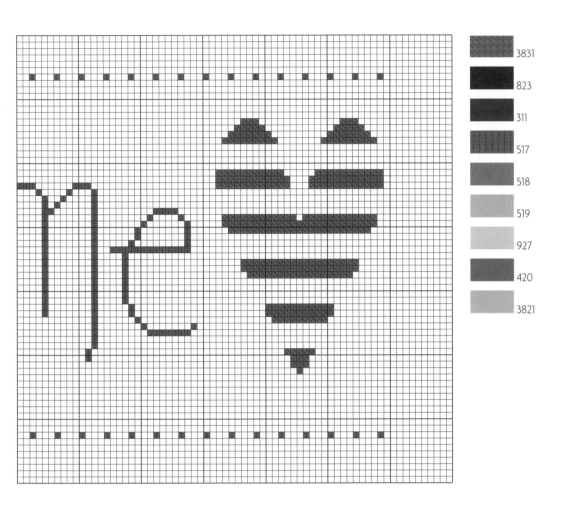

	3831
	823
	311
	517
	518
	519
	927
	420
	3821

Placement diagram

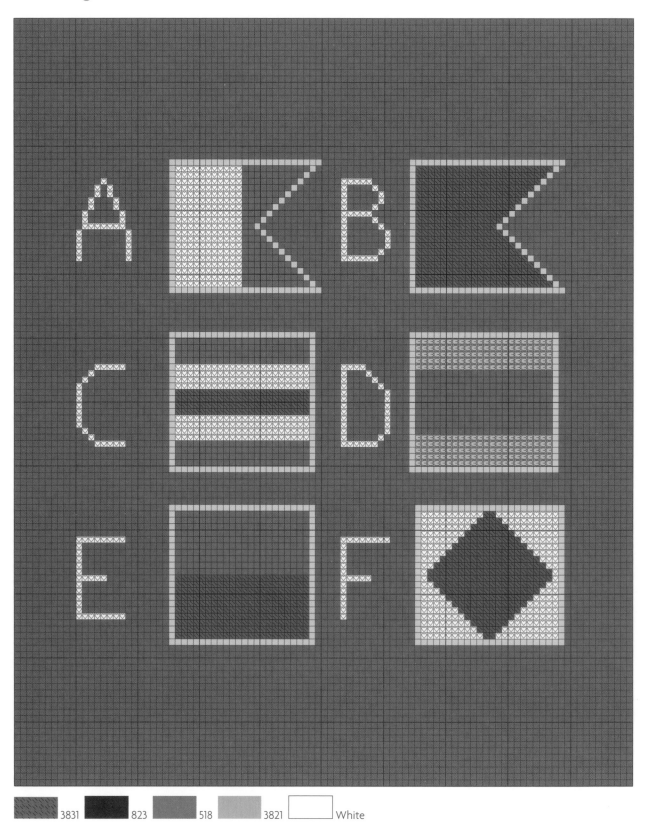

3831   823   518   3821   White

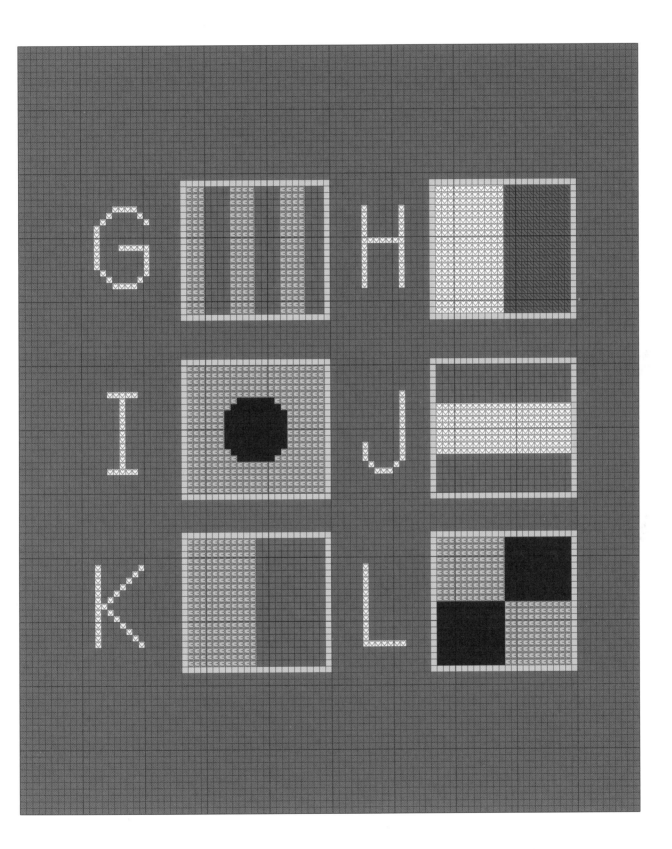

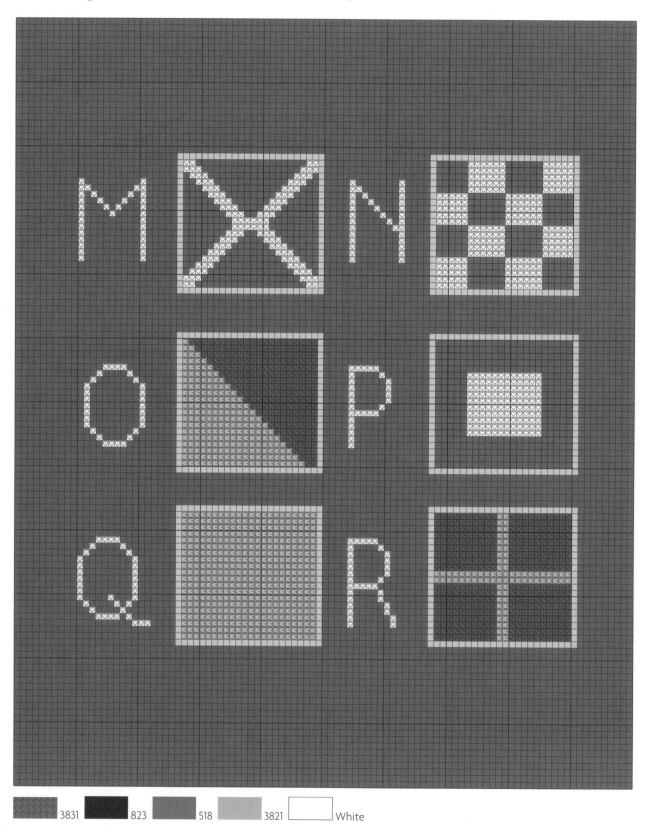

3831 823 518 3821 White

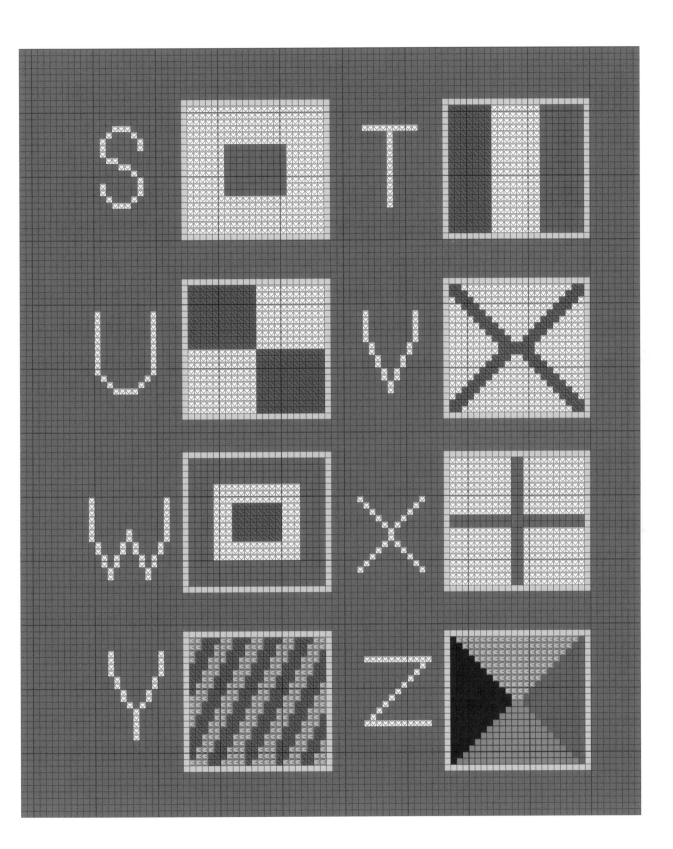

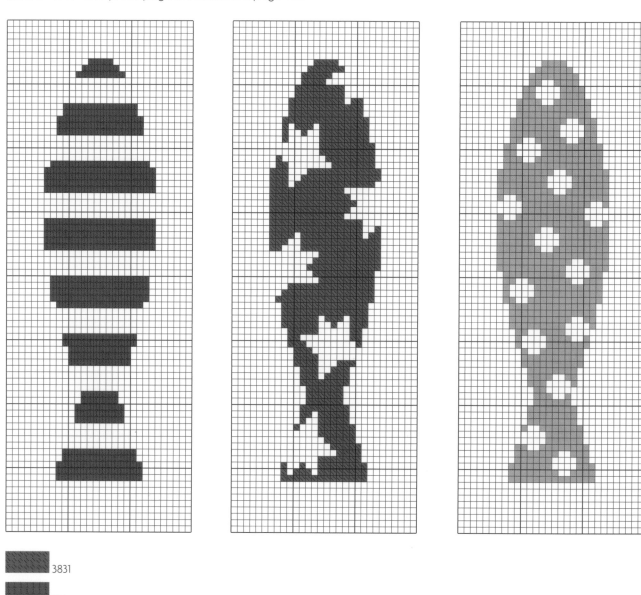

3831

517

519

	3832
	518
	519
	3761

Home chart page 67, instructions page 137

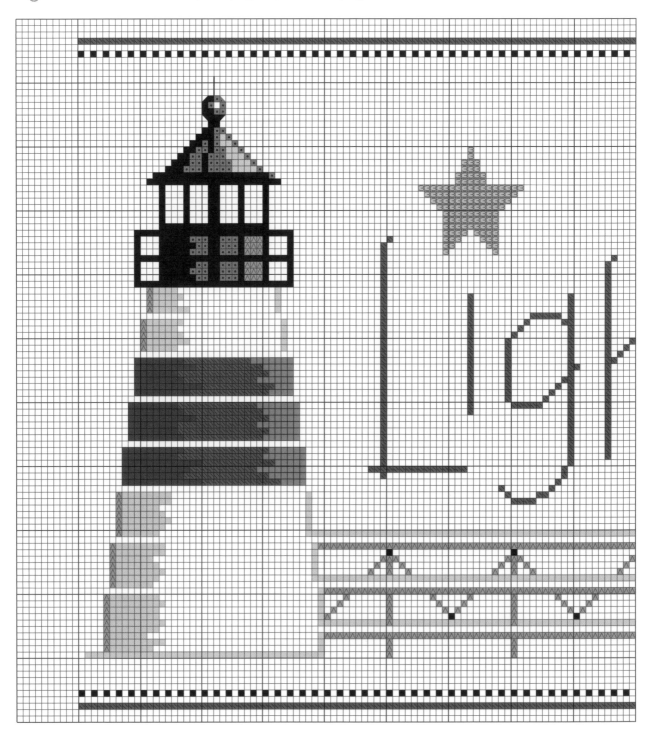

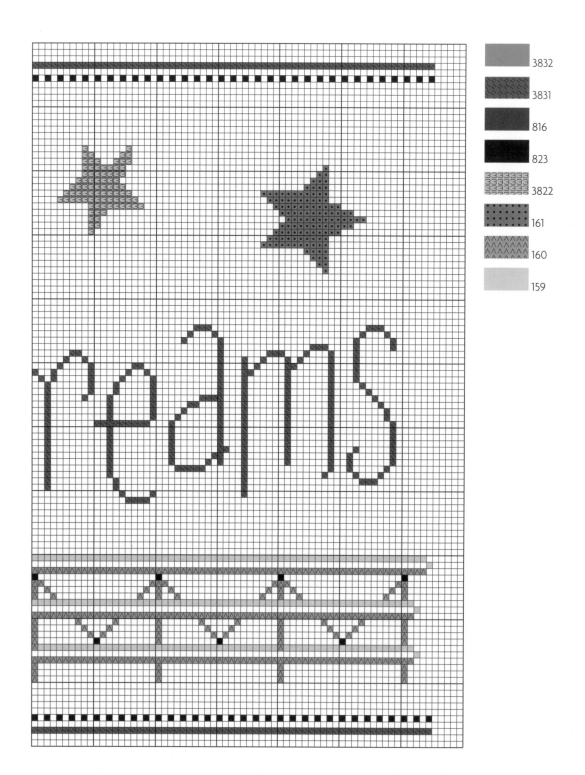

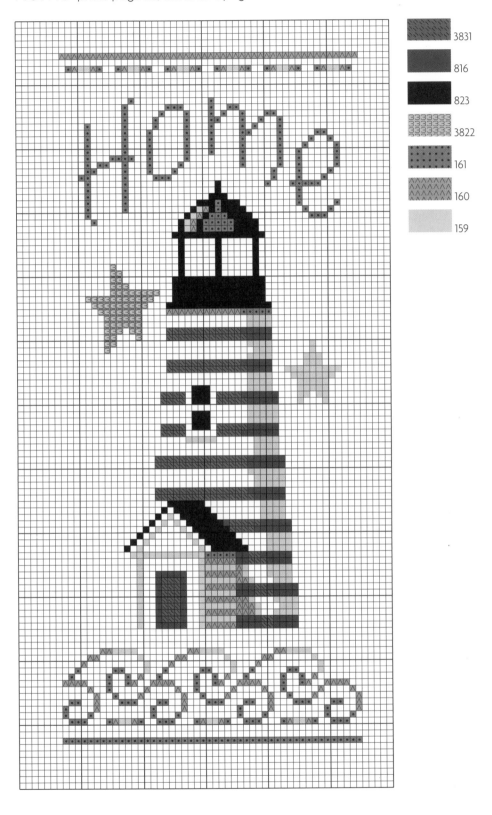

3831

816

823

3822

161

160

159

Home is where our boat is chart pages 70–71, instructions page 137

Scrapbook (detail) chart pages 70–71, instructions page 137

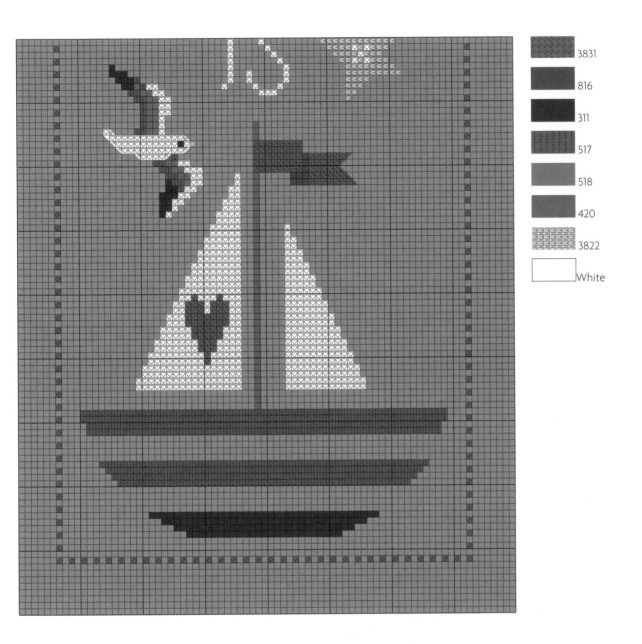

	3831
	816
	311
	517
	518
	420
	3822
	White

3831
161
160
159

	3831
	311
	161

Beach huts chart page 78, instructions page 138

Beach hut (details) charts page 79, instructions page 138

Beach huts <small>photo page 76, instructions page 138</small>

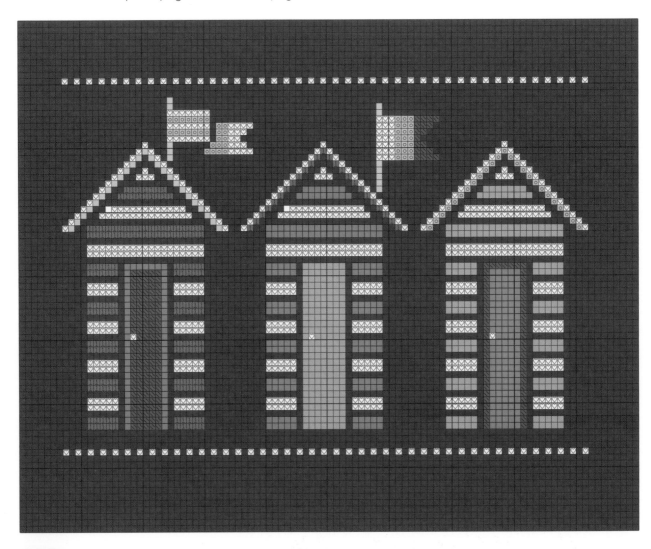

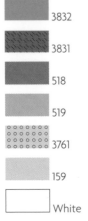

3832

3831

518

519

3761

159

White

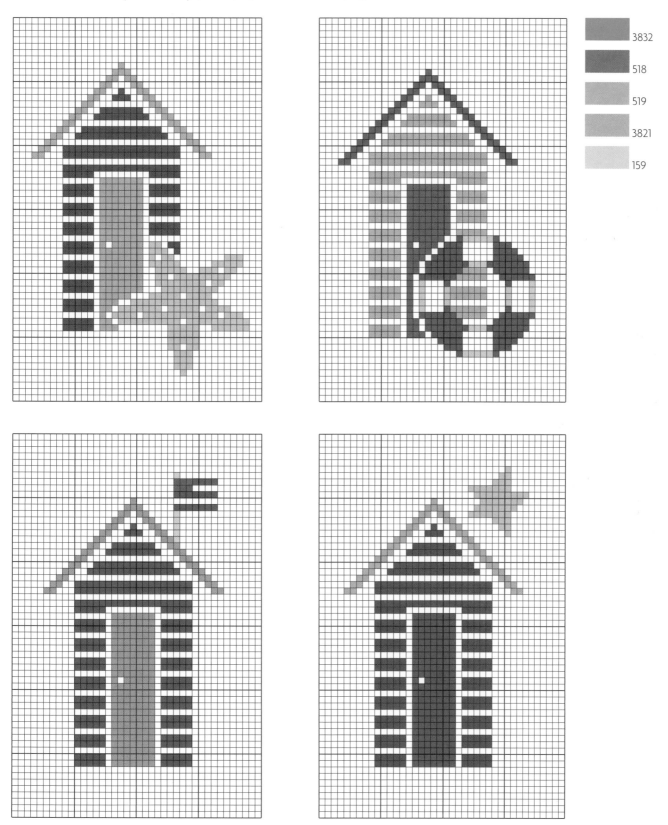

	3832
	518
	519
	3821
	159

Signpost message
chart pages 82–83, instructions page 138

January to April chart pages 88–89, instructions page 138

3832
3831
816
823
311
517
518
519
3761
3821
3822
159

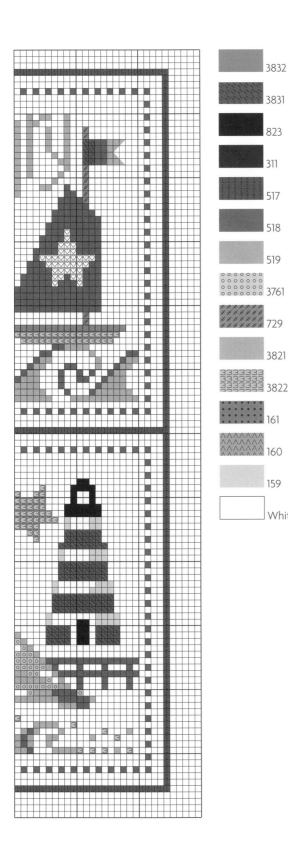

▆	3832
▨	3831
▆	823
▆	311
▦	517
▆	518
▆	519
◌	3761
▨	729
▆	3821
₃	3822
▦	161
ᐱ	160
▆	159
☐	White

Beach bag (detail) chart pages 92–93, instructions page 139

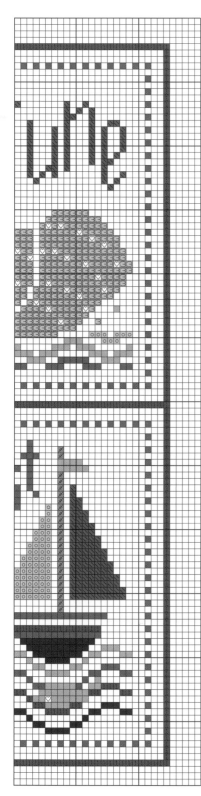

	3832
	3831
	816
	311
	517
	518
	519
	3761
	729
	3821
	3822
	White

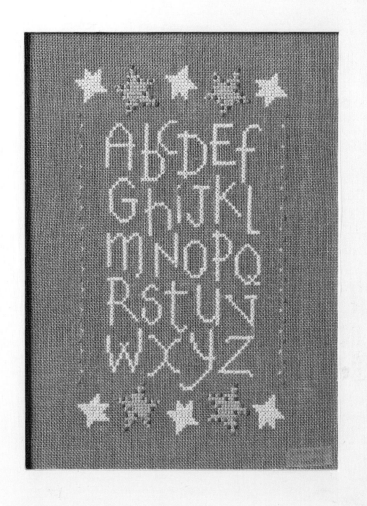

Stars pencil case (details) chart page 97, instructions page 139

3832

3831

518

159

White

Lovely boats charts pages 100–101, instructions page 139

Skippers photo pages 98–99, instructions page 139

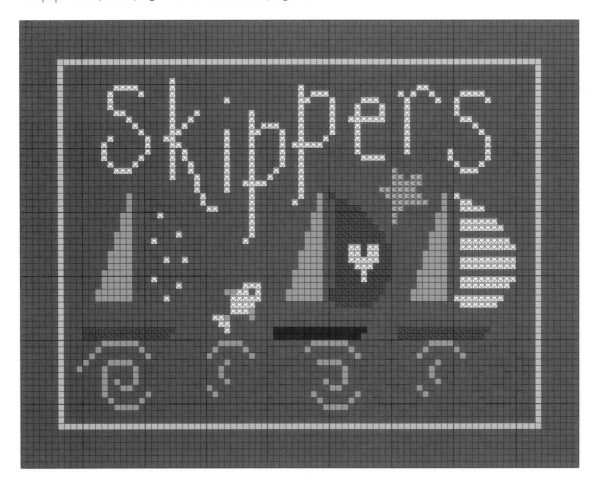

Harbour photo pages 98–99, instructions page 139

Little boat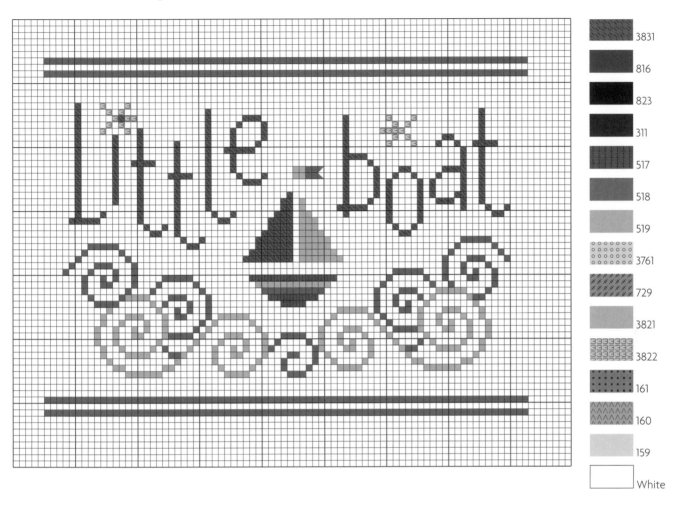

photo pages 98–99, instructions page 139

	3831
	816
	823
	311
	517
	518
	519
	3761
	729
	3821
	3822
	161
	160
	159
	White

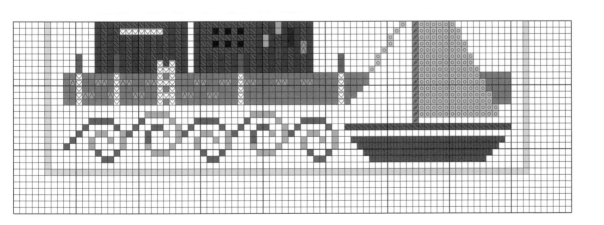

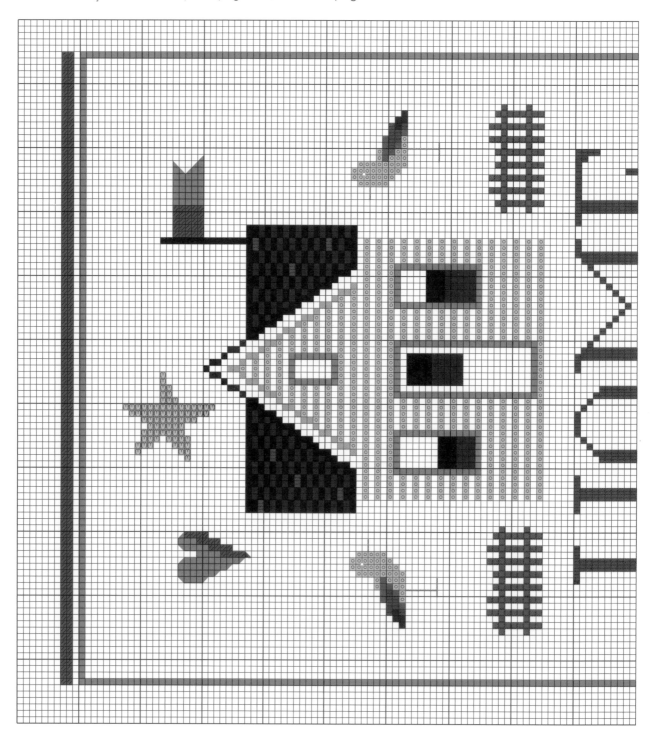

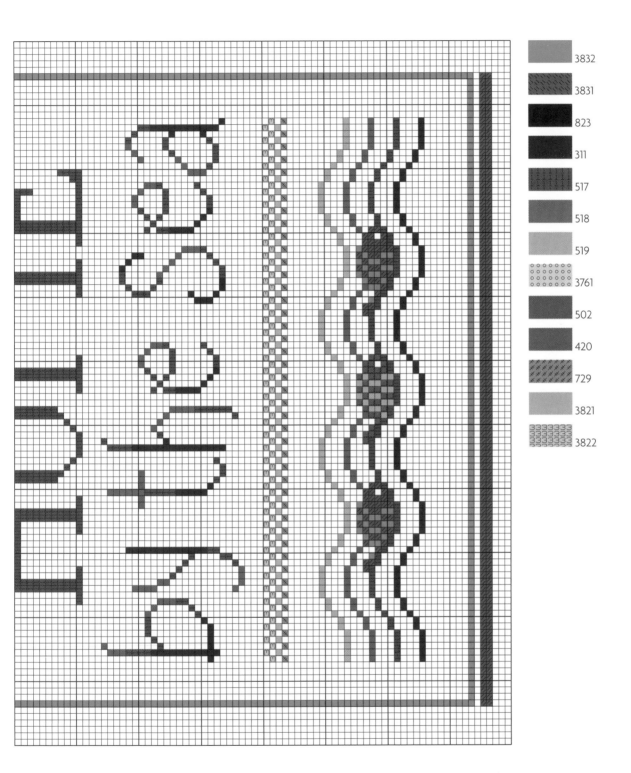

	3832
	3831
	823
	311
	517
	518
	519
	3761
	502
	420
	729
	3821
	3822

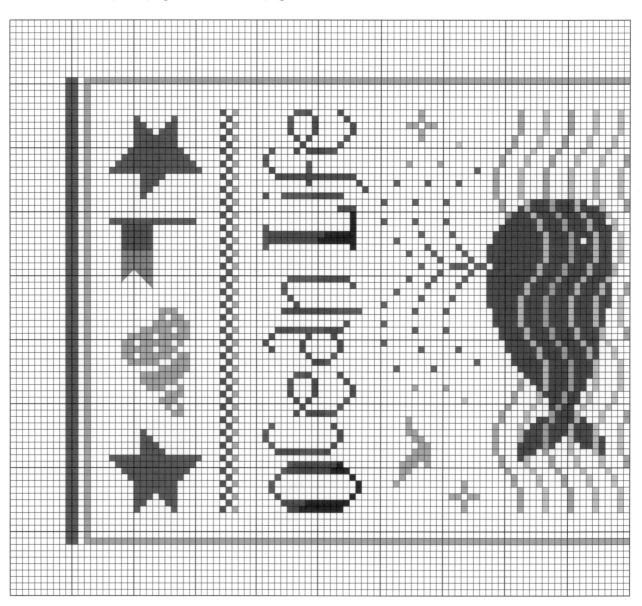

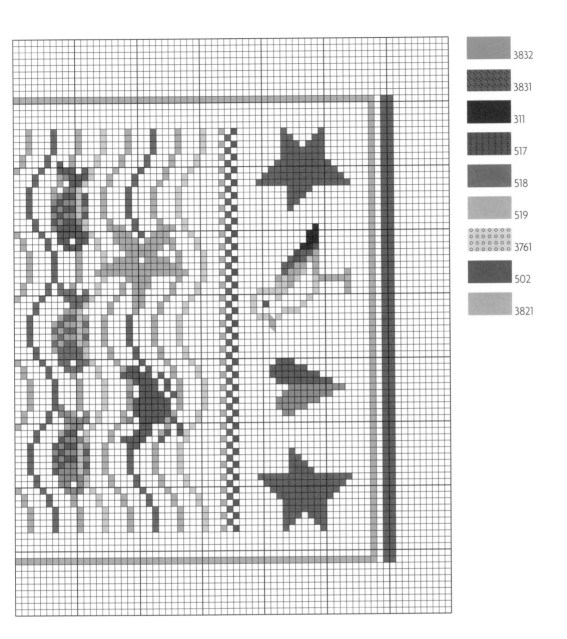

	3832
	3831
	311
	517
	518
	519
	3761
	502
	3821

September to December chart pages 112–113, instructions page 140

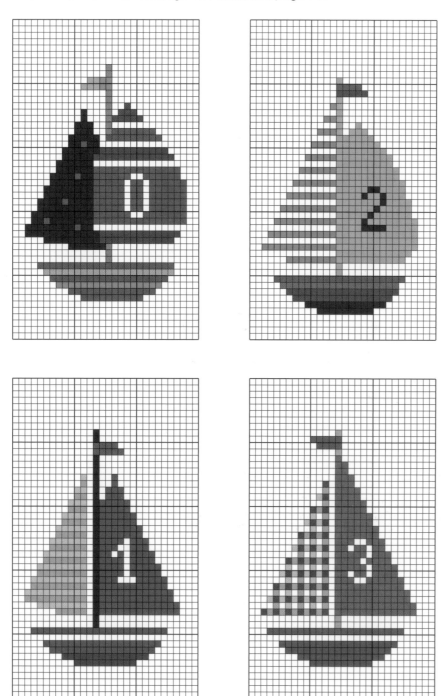

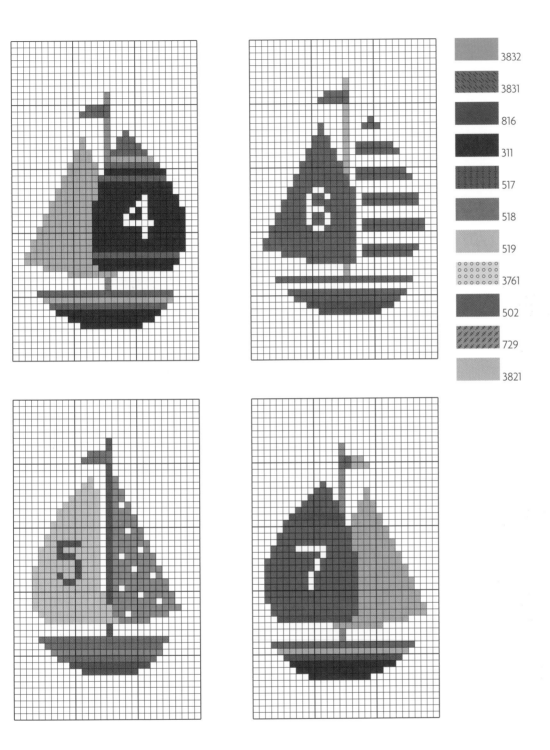

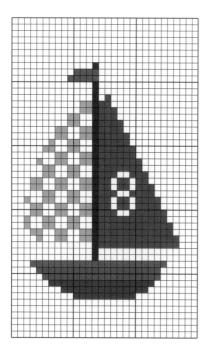

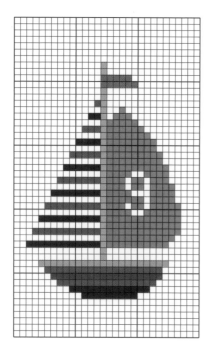

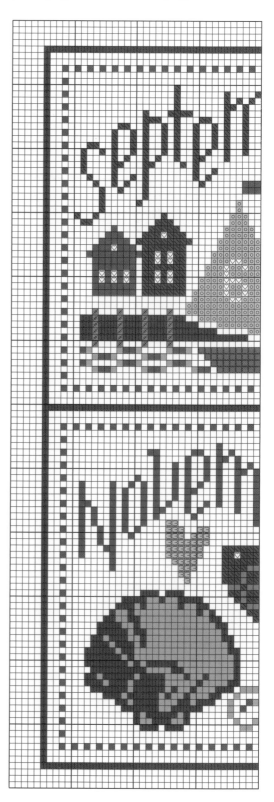

	3832
	3831
	823
	311
	517
	518
	519
	3761
	729
	3821
	3822
	161
	160
	159
	White

113

	3831
	816
	823
	311
	517
	518
	519
	3761
	3822

3831
816
823
311
517
518
519
3761
3822

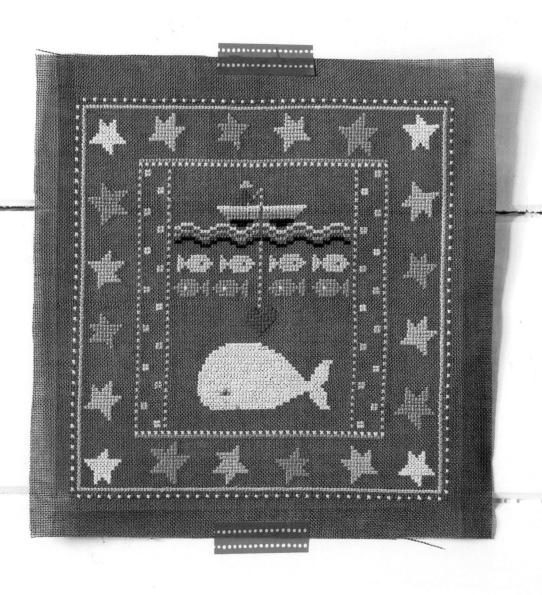

Moby Dick (detail) chart page 121, instructions page 141

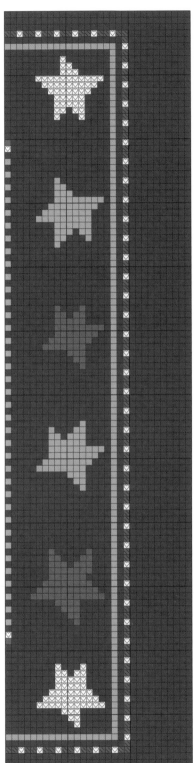

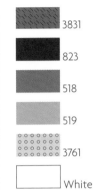

3831

823

518

519

3761

White

Moby Dick (detail) photo page 119, instructions page 141

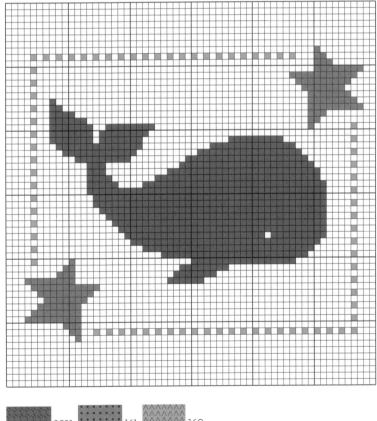

3831   161   160

abc de
fghijkLM
noPQR
STuVW
xyz
ABCDEFG
HIJKLMN
OPQRSTU
VWXYZ

3831

311

3831	
311	
517	
518	
519	
3761	

3831	311	517	518	519	3761

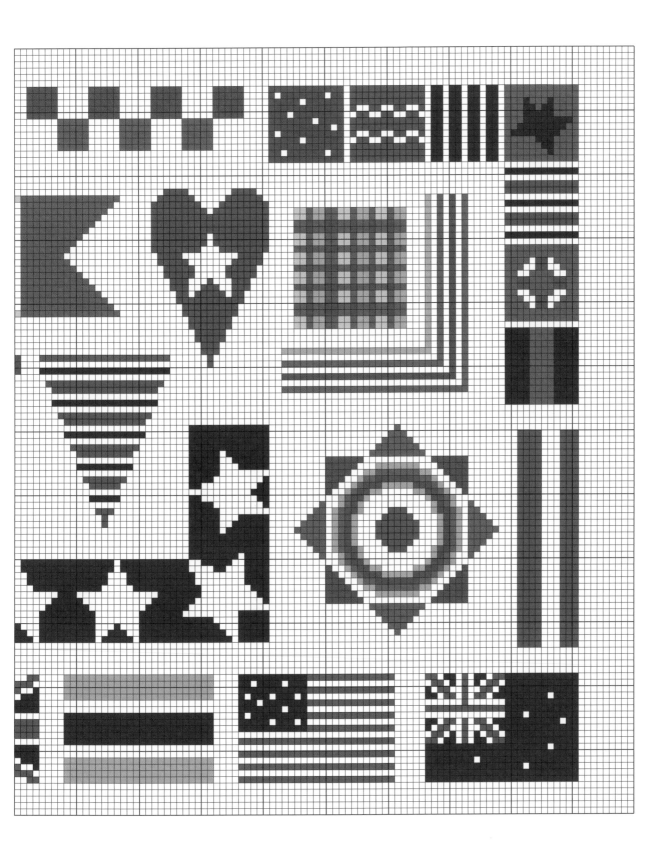

Instructions

Welcome aboard

photo page 14, chart pages 16–17
30 x 40cm (12 x 16in) piece of 30-count white linen
DMC stranded cotton (floss) 831, 311, 517, 518,
519, 3761, 160, 927, 420 and 3821
Cross stitch the design in the centre of the white linen
using two strands of thread over two threads of linen.

Visitors' book (details)

photo page 15, chart page 18
10 x 6cm (4 x 2½in) piece of 30-count
white linen canvas (for one fish)
DMC stranded cotton (floss) 3832, 3831 and 816
Cross stitch the design in the centre of the white linen
using two strands of thread over two threads of linen.
Carefully fray the edges of the fabric to give a
5mm (¼in) frayed border, then stick the cross-
stitch pieces onto the cover of the book.

Sea of liberty

photo page 20, chart page 19
22 x 28cm (8½ x 11in) piece of 30-count white linen
DMC stranded cotton (floss) 3831, 311, 517, 518,
519, 3761, 502, 501, 161, 160 and 159
Cross stitch the design in the centre of the white linen
using two strands of thread over two threads of linen.

On the seaside

photo page 21, chart pages 22–23
37 x 28cm (14½ x 11in) piece of 30-count white linen
DMC stranded cotton (floss) 3832, 3831, 816, 311,
517, 518, 519, 3761, 927, 161, 160 and 159
Cross stitch the design in the centre of the white linen
using two strands of thread over two threads of linen.

Little message (detail)
photo page 33, chart page 28
8 x 8cm (3¼ x 3¼in) piece of 30-count white linen
1 card folded in half and 1 envelope
DMC stranded cotton (floss) 3832, 3831, 816, 823, 311, 517,
518, 519, 3761, 420, 729, 3821, 3822, 161, 160, 159 plus white
Cross stitch the design in the centre of the white linen
using two strands of thread over two threads of linen.
Cut a 6.5cm (2½in) square from the centre of the card.
Stick the cross-stitch piece inside, being careful to
centre it within the cut-out square. Stick the two halves
of the card together with a few dabs of glue.

Pirate heart 1
photo page 40, chart page 42
40 x 20cm (16 x 8in) piece of 30-count white linen
25cm (10in) flax string
a little polyester fiberfill
DMC stranded cotton (floss) 816 and 311
Fold the piece of white linen in half. Cross stitch the
design in the centre of the righthand part of the fabric
using two strands of thread over two threads of linen.
Fold the fabric in half, right sides facing. Sew together, following
the line of the cross stitching, leaving an opening at the top.
Turn rights sides out and stuff the shape with a little fibrefill.
Fold the length of string in half and slip the ends into the opening
at the top of the heart. Close the opening with a few stitches.

S for ...
Surf
Sail
Sand
Sun
Sea
Shell
Swimming
Ship
photos pages 24–25, 30–31 and 32, charts pages 26–29
20 x 20cm (8 x 8in) piece of 30-count white or pale
or dark blue linen, depending on the design
DMC stranded cotton (floss) 3832, 3831, 816, 832, 311, 517,
518, 519, 3761, 420, 729, 3821, 3822, 161, 160, 159 plus white
Cross stitch the design in the centre of the linen using
two strands of thread over two threads of linen.

ABC boats

photo pages 34–35, chart pages 36–39
80 x 30cm (32 x 12in) piece of 30-count dark blue linen
DMC stranded cotton (floss) 3832, 3831, 816, 823, 311, 517, 518, 519, 3761, 420, 729, 3821, 3822, 159 plus white
Cross stitch the design in the centre of the dark blue linen using two strands of thread over two threads of linen.

Pirate heart 2

photo page 40, chart page 43
40 x 20cm (16 x 8in) piece of 20-count blue linen
25cm (10in) flax ribbon
a little polyester fiberfill
DMC stranded cotton (floss) white
Fold the piece of blue linen in half. Cross stitch the design in the centre of the righthand part of the fabric using two strands of thread over two threads of linen. Fold the fabric in half, right sides facing. Sew together, following the line of the cross stitching, leaving an opening at the top. Turn rights sides out and stuff the shape with a little fibrefill. Fold the length of ribbon in half and slip the ends into the opening at the top of the heart. Close the opening with a few stitches.

I love sea

photo page 41, chart pages 44–45
30 x 20cm (12 x 8in) piece of 30-count white linen
DMC stranded cotton (floss) 816 and 311
Cross stitch the design in the centre of the white linen using two strands of thread over two threads of linen.

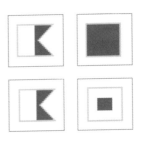

Flags (details)

photo page 52, charts pages 54–57
12 x 4cm (4½ x 1½in) piece of 30-count
white linen (for one pennant)
1 wooden skewer
DMC stranded cotton (floss) 3831, 823, 518 and 159
Cross stitch the design on the righthand part of the linen using two strands of thread over two threads of linen. Turn over the lefthand side of the fabric and hem, leaving just enough space to slide in the wooden skewer. Carefully fray the righthand edge of the flag or cut it, depending on the design.

Beach flags (detail)

photo page 53, charts pages 54–57
25 x 15cm (10 x 6in) piece of 20-count blue linen
DMC stranded cotton (floss) 3831, 823, 518 and 159
Select a word or phrase and cross stitch the letters and corresponding flags in the centre of the blue linen using two strands of thread over two threads of linen.

Sail away
photo pages 46–47, chart pages 48–51
65 x 20cm (25½ x 8in) piece of 30-count white linen
DMC stranded cotton (floss) 3831, 823, 311, 517, 518, 519, 927, 420 and 3821
Cross stitch the design in the centre of the white linen using two strands of thread over two threads of linen.

Little fishes
photo page 58, charts page 60
12 x 8cm (4½ x 3¼in) piece of 30-count white linen (for one fish)
15cm (6in) flax string, a little polyester fiberfill
DMC stranded cotton (floss) 3831, 517 and 519
Fold the piece of white linen in half. Cross stitch the design in the centre of the righthand part of the fabric using two strands of thread over two threads of linen. Fold the fabric in half, right sides facing. Sew together, following the line of the cross stitching, leaving an opening at the top. Turn rights sides out and stuff the shape with a little fibrefill. Fold the length of string in half and slip the ends into the opening at the top of the heart. Close the opening with a few stitches.

Happy little fish
photo page 59, chart page 61
20 x 27cm (8 x 10¾in) piece of 30-count white linen
DMC stranded cotton (floss) 3832, 518, 519 and 3761
Cross stitch the design in the centre of the white linen using two strands of thread over two threads of linen.

Lighthouse dreams
photo page 62, chart pages 60–66
50 x 27cm (20 x 10¾in) piece of 30-count white linen, DMC stranded cotton (floss) 3832, 3831, 816, 823, 3822, 161, 160 and 159
Cross stitch the design in the centre of the white linen using two strands of thread over two threads of linen.

Home
photo page 63, chart page 67
17 x 27cm (6½ x 10¾in) piece of 30-count white linen
DMC stranded cotton (floss) 3831, 816,
823, 3822, 161, 160 and 159
Cross stitch the design in the centre of the white linen
using two strands of thread over two threads of linen.

Home is where our boat is
photos pages 68 and 69, chart pages 70–71
22 x 45cm (8¾ x 17¾in) piece of 30-count blue linen
DMC stranded cotton (floss) 3831, 816, 311,
517, 518, 420, 3822 plus white
Cross stitch the design in the centre of the dark blue linen
using two strands of thread over two threads of linen.

Scrapbook (detail)
photo page 69, chart page 71
37 x 61cm (14½ x 24in) piece of 30-count white linen
1 A4 (US-letter-sized) notebook
DMC stranded cotton (floss) 3831, 816, 311, 517, 518 plus white
Fold the piece of linen in half. Make two 6cm (2½in) flaps,
allowing 3cm (1¼in) seam allowance. Cross stitch the
design in the centre of the righthand part of the fabric
using two strands of thread over two threads of linen. Hem
3cm (1¼in) around all the edges. Seam the flaps.

Hello captain
photo page 74, chart page 72
20 x 25cm (8 x 10in) piece of 30-count white linen
DMC stranded cotton (floss) 3831, 161, 160 and 159
Cross stitch the design in the centre of the white linen
using two strands of thread over two threads of linen.

Welcome home sailor
photo page 75, chart page 73
20 x 25cm (8 x 10in) piece of 30-count white linen
DMC stranded cotton (floss) 3831, 311 and 161
Cross stitch the design in the centre of the white linen
using two strands of thread over two threads of linen.

Beach huts
photo page 76, chart page 78
25 x 20cm (10 x 8in) piece of 30-count dark blue linen
DMC stranded cotton (floss) 3832, 3831,
518, 519, 3761, 159 plus white
Cross stitch the design in the centre of the dark blue linen
using two strands of thread over two threads of linen.

Beach huts (detail)
photo page 77, charts page 79
8 x 11cm (3¼ x 4¼in) piece of 30-count white linen
1 cushion and 1 blue cushion cover,
each 45 x 30cm (17¾ x 12in)
DMC stranded cotton (floss) 3832, 518, 519, 3821 and 159
Cross stitch the design in the centre of the white linen using
two strands of thread over two threads of linen. Fold over
the edges of the cross-stitch piece. Sew the piece onto
the top left of the cushion cover using running stitches.

January to April
photo page 85, chart pages 88–89
30 x 30cm (12 x 12in) piece of 30-count white linen
DMC stranded cotton (floss) 3832, 3831, 823, 311, 517, 518,
519, 3761, 729, 3821, 3822, 161, 160, 159 plus white
Cross stitch the design in the centre of the white linen triangles
using two strands of thread over two threads of linen.

May to August
photo page 85, chart pages 92–93
30 x 30 cm piece of 30-count white linen
DMC stranded cotton (floss) 3832, 3831, 816, 311, 517, 518,
519, 3761, 729, 3821, 3822 plus white
Cross stitch the design in the centre of the white linen
using two strands of thread over two threads of linen.

Message sign
photo pages 80–81, chart pages 82–83
33 x 10cm (13 x 4in) piece of 30-count white linen
1 rectangle of white fabric 5mm (¼in) smaller on
each side than the size of the cross-stitch piece
1 piece of wood 2cm (¾in) smaller on
each side than the cross-stitch
15cm (6in) white ribbon
DMC stranded cotton (floss) 3831, 311 and 517
Cross stitch the design in the centre of the linen using two
strands of thread over two threads of linen. Place the cross-
stitch piece on the wood and staple on the back. Staple the
ribbon ends on the back of the sign, halfway between each
end and the centre. Turn over the edges of the white fabric
5mm (¼in) on each side and glue in place on the back of
the sign. If you want to put a different message, start by cross
stitching it in the centre of the linen. Next cross stitch the arrow
point, then the horizontal lines, finishing with the vertical one.

Lighthouse ABC

photo page 84, chart pages 86–87
20 x 40cm (8 x 16in) piece
of 30-count white linen
DMC stranded cotton (floss) 3831,
3832, 816, 823, 311, 517, 518,
519, 3761, 3821, 3822 and 159
Cross stitch the design in the centre
of the white linen using two strands
of thread over two threads of linen.

Star pencil case

photo page 95, chart page 97
20 x 20cm (8 x 8 in) piece of 30-count white linen
1 x 18cm (7in) zipper
DMC stranded cotton (floss) 3831 and 518
Cross stitch a stars design on the top half of the linen using
two strands of thread over two threads of linen.
Hem 1cm (½in) at the top and bottom of the piece of linen.
Fold the fabric in half, right sides facing. Stitch together
the sides, turn right sides out and sew in the zipper.

Beach bag (detail)

photo page 91, chart pages 92–93
20 x 10cm (8 x 4in) piece of 30-count white linen
1 white canvas bag
DMC stranded cotton (floss) 3832, 3831 and 816
Cross stitch the design in the centre of the white linen
using two strands of thread over two threads of linen. Stitch
the cross-stitch piece onto the front of the bag. You can
customize it by overstitching the handle details in red.

ABC stars

photo page 94, chart page 96
20 x 30cm (8 x 12in) piece of 30-count blue-grey linen
DMC stranded cotton (floss) 3832, 3831, 518, 159 plus white
Cross stitch a stars design on the top half of the linen
using two strands of thread over two threads of linen.

Skippers

photo pages 95–96, chart page 100

Harbour

photo pages 95–96, charts pages 100–101

Little boat

photo pages 95–96, chart page 101
22 x 20 cm (8½ x 8in) piece of 30-count white or
dark blue linen, depending on the design
DMC stranded cotton (floss) 3831, 816, 823, 311, 517, 518,
519, 3761, 729, 3821, 3822, 161, 160, 159 plus white
Cross stitch the design in the centre of the linen using
two strands of thread over two threads of linen.

Home by the sea
photo page 102, chart pages 104–105
22 x 30cm (8½ x 12in) piece of 30-count white linen
DMC stranded cotton (floss) 3832, 3831, 823, 311, 517,
518, 519, 3761, 502, 420, 729, 3821 and 3822
Cross stitch the design in the centre of the white linen
using two strands of thread over two threads of linen.

Ocean life
photo page 103, chart pages 106–107
20 x 35cm (8 x 14in) piece of 30-count white linen
DMC stranded cotton (floss) 3832, 3831, 311,
517, 518, 519, 3761, 502 and 3821
Cross stitch the design in the centre of the white linen
using two strands of thread over two threads of linen.

From 0 to 9
photo page 108, charts pages 110–112
1m x 50cm (40 x 20in) piece of 30-count white linen
3.5m (3¾yds) white cotton bias binding
DMC stranded cotton (floss) 3832, 3831, 816, 311,
517, 518, 519, 3761, 502, 729 and 3821
Cut nine triangles from the white linen, each with a base of
23cm (9in) and two sides of 25cm (10in). Hem 1cm (½in)
around all the edges. Cross stitch the design in the centre of
the white linen using two strands of thread over two threads of
linen. Lay the cross-stitched triangles down in front of you. Fold
the bias binding in half and pin along each side of the bases
of the triangles from 0 to 9, spreading them out along the
bias strip and leaving 1m (40in) at each end. Sew in place.

September to December
photo page 109
chart pages 112–113
30 x 30cm (12 x 12 in) piece
of 30-count white linen
DMC stranded cotton (floss)
3832, 3831, 823, 311, 517,
518, 519, 3761, 729, 3821,
3822, 161, 160, 159 plus white
Cross stitch the design in
the centre of the white
linen triangles using two
strands of thread over
two threads of linen.

Little houses 1
photo page 114, chart page 116
20 x 25cm (8 x 10in) piece
of 30-count white linen
DMC stranded cotton (floss) 3831, 816,
823, 311, 517, 518, 519, 3761 and 3822
Cross stitch the design in the centre of
the white linen triangles using two strands
of thread over two threads of linen.

Little houses 2
photo page 115, chart page 117
20 x 25cm (8 x 10in) piece
of 30-count white linen
DMC stranded cotton (floss) 3831, 816,
823, 311, 517, 518, 519, 3761 and 3822
Cross stitch the design in the centre
of the white linen using two strands of
thread over two threads of linen.

ABC seagulls
photo page 122, chart page 125
20 x 25cm (8 x 10in) piece
of 30-count white linen
DMC stranded cotton (floss) 3831,
311, 517, 518, 519 and 3761
Cross stitch the design in the centre
of the white linen using two strands
of thread over two threads of linen.

Good catch
photo page 119, chart pages 120–121
25 x 25cm (10 x 10in) piece of 30-count dark blue linen
DMC stranded cotton (floss), 3831, 823, 518, 519, 3761 plus white
Cross stitch the design in the centre of the white linen
using two strands of thread over two threads of linen.

Maritime medley
photo pages 128–129, charts pages 126–127
Two 58 x 45cm (22¾ x 17¾in) pieces of 30-count white linen
1 rectangular cushion 55 x 43cm (22½ x 17in)
1 x 30cm (12in) zipper
DMC stranded cotton (floss) 3831, 311, 517, 518, 519 and 3761
Cross stitch the design in the centre of the linen using two
strands of thread over two threads of linen. Pin the two linen
rectangles right sides facing and sew together 1.5cm (⅝in) in
from the edges, leaving a 30cm (12in) opening along one side.
Turn the cushion cover right sides out and sew in the zipper.

Moby Dick (detail)
photo page 119, chart page 121
12 x 12cm (8 x 8in) piece of
30-count white linen
1 red canvas bag
DMC stranded cotton (floss)
3831, 160 and 161
Cross stitch the design in the centre
of the white linen using two strands
of thread over two threads of linen.
Sew the cross-stitched piece onto
the centre of the red canvas bag.

ABC fish
photo pages 122–123
chart page 124
20 x 25cm (8 x 10in) piece
of 30-count white linen
DMC stranded cotton
(floss) 3831 and 311
Cross stitch the design in the centre
of the white linen using two strands
of thread over two threads of linen.

This is the end
photo page 142, charts pages 54–57
10 x 20cm (4 x 8in) piece of 30-count white linen
DMC stranded cotton (floss) 3831, 518, 3822 and 159
Cross stitch the design in the centre of the white linen
using two strands of thread over two threads of linen.

Acknowledgments

Thanks to Julianne, Ryan and Emma. Thanks to Mary, who was my guide from Boston to Freeport. Thanks to Lise and Fred for their helpful observations, thanks to Dominique, and thanks to Pascale for so many things.

A big thank you to Laurence, the owner of the beautiful gîtes *La Maison sur le quai* and *Un bateau sous mon transat* at Port–en–Bessin for her friendly welcome and her availability.

www.lamaisonsurlequai.com

www.unbateausousmontransat.org

Suppliers

Stitch Craft Create
www.stitchcraftcreate.co.uk

La Croix and la Manière
36, rue Faidherbe
75011 Paris
www. lacroixetlamaniere.com

Mercerie Mouline
2, 4, 6, rue Livingstone
75018 Paris
www.moline–mercerie.com

Tissus Reine
3, 5, place Saint–Pierre
75018 Paris
www.tissus–reine.com

Déballage Dreyfus
Marché Saint–Pierre
2, rue Charles–Noguier
75018 Paris
www.marchesaintpierre.com

Mercerie Rascol
www.rascol.com

Mercerie La Couserie créative
www.lacouseriecreative.com

Ma Petite Mercerie
www.mapetitemercerie.com

Index

This is the end charts pages 54–57, instructions page 135

A DAVID & CHARLES BOOK
© Marabout (Hachette Livre) 2012
43, quai de Grenelle, 75905 Paris Cedex 15

David & Charles is an imprint of F&W Media International, LTD
Brunel House, Forde Close, Newton Abbot, TQ12 4PU, UK

F&W Media International, LTD is a subsidiary of F+W Media In
10151 Carver Road, Suite #200, Blue Ash, OH 45242, USA

Originally published in France as *Bord de Mer*
First published in the UK and US in 2013 by F&W Media
International, LTD

Anna Field has asserted her right to be identified as author
of this work in accordance with the Copyright, Designs and
Patents Act, 1988.

A catalogue record for this book is available from the British
Library.

ISBN-13: 978-1-4463-0322-1 paperback
ISBN-10: 1-4463-0322-5 paperback

Design and layout: Frédéric Voisin

Printed in China by RR Donnelley
for F&W Media International, LTD
Brunel House, Forde Close, Newton Abbot, TQ12 4PU, UK

F+W Media Inc. publishes high-quality books on a wide rang
of subjects. For more great ideas visit:
www.stitchcraftcreate.co.uk